First published by Affirm Press in 2025
Bunurong/Boon Wurrung Country
28 Thistlethwaite Street
South Melbourne VIC 3205
affirmpress.com.au

Affirm Press is located on the unceded land of the Bunurong/Boon Wurrung peoples of the Kulin Nation. Affirm Press pays respect to their Elders past and present.

1 3 5 7 9 10 8 6 4 2

A catalogue record for this book is available from the National Library of Australia

ISBN: 9781923022690 (hardback)

Cover and internal design based on the series design by Steph Spartels © Affirm Press
Cover illustrations by Christine Cuddihy © Christine Cuddihy
Proudly printed and bound in China by RR Donnelley Asia Printing Solutions Ltd

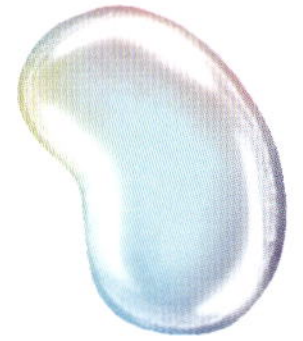

YOUR BODY IS AMAZING

Jess Sanders with art by Christine Cuddihy

Dear Reader,

There is no such thing as a perfect body. Every body is different and every body has its own strengths. What makes your body amazing is not what it looks like, but what it allows you to do.

It is my hope that you and your body get to experience all the wonderful things this world has to offer.

Your friend,

Jess

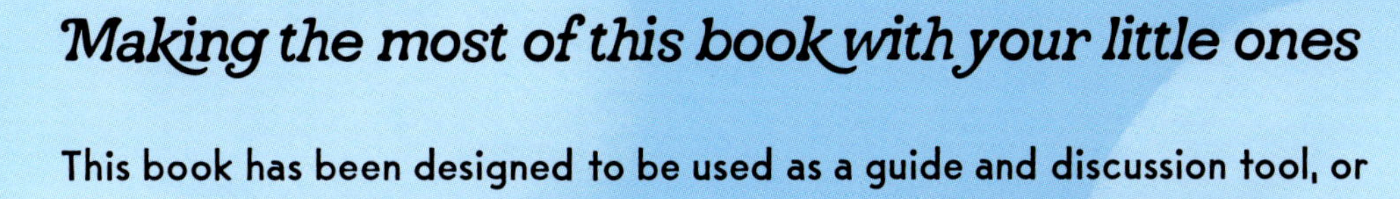

Making the most of this book with your little ones

This book has been designed to be used as a guide and discussion tool, or simply as a story about appreciating your body and understanding that you are so much more than what your body looks like. Whichever way you use this book, I hope you and your little one come away knowing that your body is amazing, exactly as it is.

Having conversations about body image and body esteem can be tricky, which is why there are some examples and suggestions in the book to organically invite little ones to reflect on their own experiences.

Your little one needs to know that they are not alone in their feelings, so giving age-appropriate examples of your own experience as a child and as a grown-up will help you both navigate these life lessons together.

If you'd like to explore more ways to unpack this topic, each *Life Lessons for Little Ones* book is supported by specially designed discussion questions available at www.jesssanders.com.au

Jess Sanders is a social worker and best-selling, award-winning author who specialises in supporting young people. Jess has a passion for creating resources that nurture positive mental health and promote gender equality.

For Dad,

For always being there.

Love, Jess

Your body is not too small,
and it is not too big.
It is not too short,
and it is not too tall.

Your body is actually amazing.

Just as it is.

Bodies come in all different shapes and sizes, and there is no such thing as a 'perfect' body.

What makes your body amazing is not what it **looks** like.
What makes your body amazing is what it can **do**!

Your body is super smart,
and it is always looking out for you.

When you eat, your body turns food into energy so that you can grow and learn and play.

When you are sick, your body does everything it can to help you get better.

When you sleep, your body recharges so that you can enjoy a new day.

Your body is also your home, and it allows you to experience all the incredible things that life has to offer.

Your body allows you to taste and smell your favourite foods,

watch your favourite movies,

hear your favourite songs,

play your favourite games,

and hug your favourite people.

Every body is amazing in its own way,
and every body has its own incredible abilities and strengths.

Your body might be able to reach a high shelf,
or it might be able to squeeze into small spaces.

Your body might be great at sport or talented at dance!

And your body might be super strong or flexible.

But sometimes you might forget
that your body is amazing.

You might compare your body to others
or feel frustrated that your body doesn't do the
things you want it to do. It's normal to feel
this way from time to time.

You might also find yourself feeling uncomfortable in your body as it changes and grows.

This is normal too. Your body will change throughout your life. In fact, it has already changed a lot since you were born!

There are things you can do to care for your body and remind yourself of how amazing it truly is.

You could move your body in a way that feels good for you.

You could eat yummy foods that make your body feel nourished.

You could rest when your body feels tired.

You could write a list of all the things your body allows you to do.

You could look in the mirror and say to yourself, 'My body is amazing, and so am I!'

And you can always talk to a trusted grown-up
about how you are feeling.

Your body is always working hard for you, and it is your home for life.

Try to take care of your body as best you can and celebrate your body every day so that it can keep doing amazing things.

You can do this by eating nourishing food, moving each day, resting when you are tired, and reminding yourself of all the incredible things your body can do.

Your body is one of a kind.

Your body is yours for life.

Your body is amazing!

Visit www.jesssanders.com.au for more resources for your little ones.

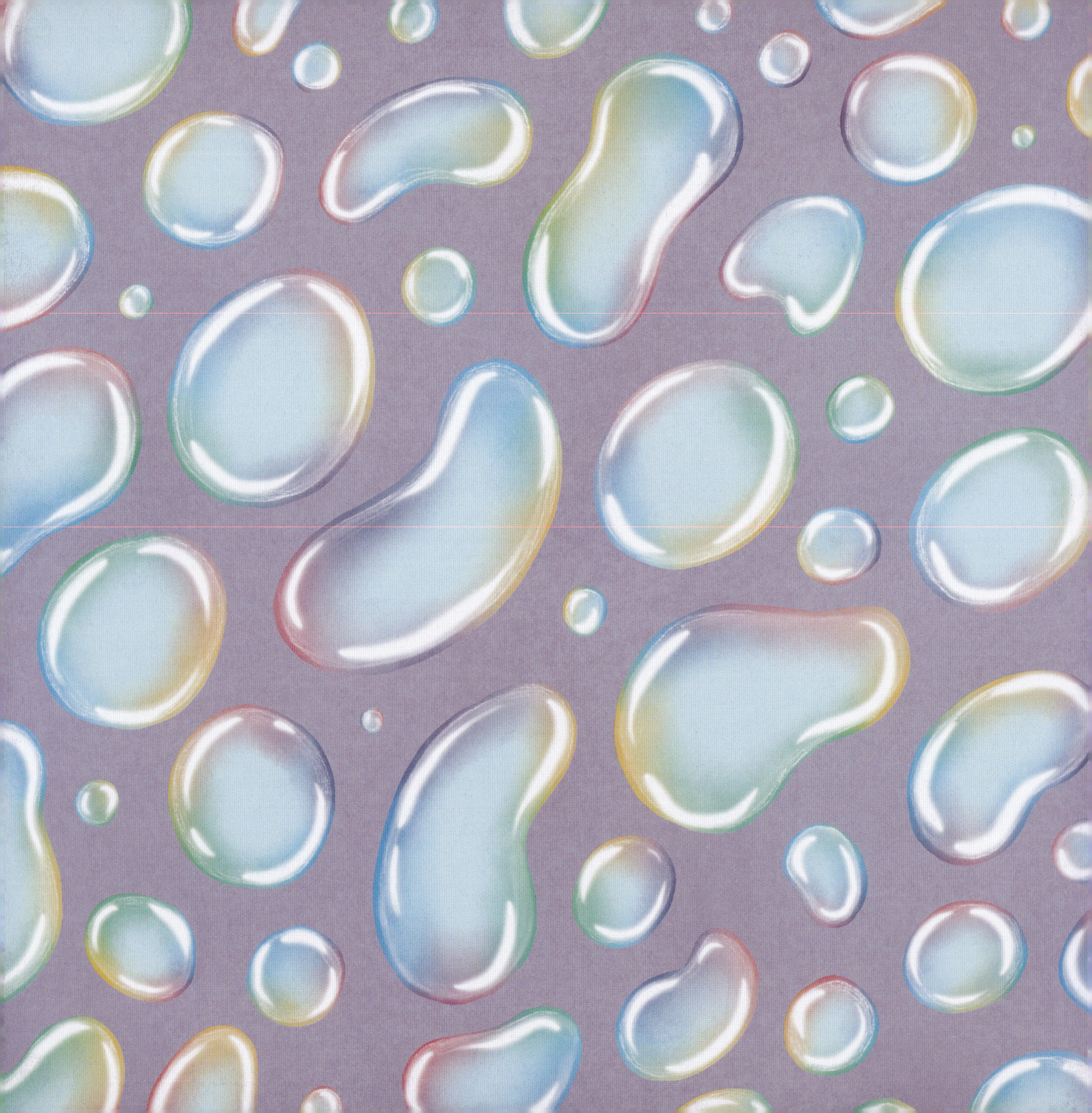